WEST OF THE MOON

SENIOR AUTHOR

JACK BOOTH

DAVID BOOTH

WILLA PAULI & JO PHENIX

IMPRESSIONS

HOLT, RINEHART AND WINSTON OF CANADA, LIMITED

Senior Editor: Wendy Cochran
Developmental Editor: Deborah Gordon Lewi
Production Editor: Jocelyn Van Huyse
Design: Wycliffe Smith
Art Direction: Holly Fisher
Cover Illustrator: Heather Cooper

ISBN: 0-03-921456-7

Canadian Cataloguing in Publication Data

Main entry under title:
West of the Moon

(Impressions)
For use in schools.
ISBN 0-03-921456-7

1. Readers (Primary).   2. Readers – 1950 –
I. Booth, Jack, 1946 –   II. Series.

PE1119.W53   428.6   C83-098251-5

Illustrations
Jock MacRae: pp. 6-7, 47, 205; *Joanne Fitzgerald:* pp. 8-9, 80-81, 228-238; *Dr. Seuss:* pp. 10-16; *Lisa Smith:* pp. 17, 136, 145, 156-157, 180-181; *Debi Perna:* pp. 18-24; *Clive Dobson:* pp. 25, 98-99, 165, 239-242; *Barbara Klunder:* pp. 26-35; 206-207; *Arnold Lobel:* 36-46, 182-189; *William Kimber:* pp. 48-49; *Magda Markowski:* pp. 50, 118-123; *Maurice Sendak:* pp. 51-55; *Graham Bardell:* pp. 56-57; *Greg Ruhl:* pp. 58-79; *Frank Hammond:* pp. 82-85; *Sami Suomalainen:* pp. 86-88; *Nancy Lou Reynolds:* pp. 89-97; *Loris Lesynski:* pp. 100-101; *San Murata:* pp. 102-113; *Joe Weissmann:* pp. 114-117; *Brenda Clark:* pp. 124-128; *Sue Wilkinson:* pp. 129-135; *Katrin Brandt:* pp. 137-144; *Jack Newnham:* pp. 146-155; *Lillian Hoban:* pp. 158-164; *Leslie Fairfield:* pp. 166-175; *James Marshall:* pp. 176-179; *Sylvie Daigneault:* pp. 190-191, 208-217; *Thomas Di Grazia:* pp. 192-204; *Chris Workman:* pp. 218-219; *Demi:* pp. 220-225; *Frank Viva:* pp. 226-227; *Wallace Tripp:* pp. 243-245; *Ron Berg:* pp. 246-255, 256.

The authors and publishers gratefully acknowledge the consultants listed below for their contribution to the development of this program:

Isobel Bryan   *Primary Consultant   Ottawa Board of Education*
Ethel Buchanan   *Language Arts Consultant   Winnipeg, Manitoba*
Heather Hayes   *Elementary Curriculum Consultant   City of Halifax Board of Education*
Gary Heck   *Curriculum Co-ordinator, Humanities   Lethbridge School District No. 51*
Ina Mary Rutherford   *Supervisor of Reading and Primary Instruction   Bruce County Board of Education*
Janice M. Sarkissian   *Supervisor of Instruction (Primary and Pre-School)   Greater Victoria School District*
Lynn Taylor   *Language Arts Consultant   Saskatoon Catholic School Board*

Printed in Canada   6 7 8 9   91 90 89 88 87

Acknowledgements

Help!: In THE SNOPP ON THE SIDEWALK AND OTHER POEMS by Jack Prelutsky. Copyright © 1976, 1977 by Jack Prelutsky. By permission of Greenwillow Books (A Division of William Morrow & Company). *I Can Lick 30 Tigers Today!*: From I CAN LICK 30 TIGERS TODAY AND OTHER STORIES, by Dr. Seuss. Copyright © 1969 by Dr. Seuss. Reprinted by permission of Random House, Inc. *Who to Pet and Who Not to*: From X.J. Kennedy, ONE WINTER NIGHT IN AUGUST, AND OTHER NONSENSE JINGLES. Copyright © 1975 by X.J. Kennedy. A Margaret K. McElderry book. (New York: Atheneum, 1975) Reprinted with permission of Atheneum Publishers and Curtis Brown Ltd. *Mine Will, Said John*: By Helen V. Griffith. (entire text, no illustrations) Text copyright © 1967 by Helen V. Griffith. By permission of Greenwillow Books (A Division of William Morrow & Company). *Like a Giant in a Towel*: Copyright © 1974, by Dennis Lee. Reprinted by permission of Macmillan of Canada (A Division of Gage Publishing Limited). *The Hungry Thing*: From THE HUNGRY THING by Jan Slepian and Ann Seidler. Copyright © 1967 by Jan Slepian and Ann Seidler. Reprinted by permission of Modern Curriculum Press, Cleveland, Ohio. *Dinosaur Time*: Specified pages of art and text in DINOSAUR TIME by Peggy Parish. Pictures by Arnold Lobel. Text copyright © 1974 by Margaret Parish. Illustrations copyright © 1974 by Arnold Lobel. Reprinted by permission of Harper & Row, Publishers Inc. *Company*: By Bobbi Katz. © Bobbi Katz, 1971. *There Is a Place*: In EATS by Arnold Adoff. Copyright © 1979 by Arnold Adoff. By permission of Lothrop, Lee & Shepard Books (A Division of William Morrow & Company). *Little Bear Goes to the Moon*: In LITTLE BEAR by Else Holmelund Minarik, Pictures by Maurice Sendak (text and specified illustrations). Text Copyright © 1957 by Else Holmelund Minarik. Pictures Copyright © 1957 by Maurice Sendak. By permission of Harper & Row, Publishers, Inc. *Daniel's Duck*: Text of DANIEL'S DUCK by Clyde Robert Bulla. Text copyright © 1979 by Clyde Robert Bulla. By permission of Harper & Row, Publishers, Inc. *The Gentle Giant*: By Dennis Lee from JELLY BELLY by Dennis Lee. Reprinted by permission of Macmillan of Canada and The Blackie Publishing Group. *Reggie Alone*: By Shirley Benton Kerr. Copyright © 1974. All rights reserved. Published by permission of the author. *Barn Owl*: Text excerpt from BARN OWL by Phyllis Flower. Text copyright © 1978 by Phyllis Flower. A Science I CAN READ Book. By Michael Rosen from MIND YOUR OWN BUSINESS. Reprinted by permission of the publisher André Deutsch Limited. *What Did You Put in Your Pocket?*: Slightly adapted and reprinted by permission of Harcourt Brace Jovanovich, Inc. from SOMETHINGK SPECIAL, © 1958, by Beatrice de Regniers. *Spring*: (text only) from OUT IN THE DARK AND DAYLIGHT, by Aileen Fisher. Text copyright © 1980 by Aileen Fisher. Reprinted by permission of Harper & Row, Publishers, Inc. *The Caterpillar's Story*: By Achim Broger, illustrations by Katrin Brandt is reproduced by permission of The Bodley Head. *Boss for a Week*: Published by Ashton Scholastic Limited NZ. Text copyright © 1982 by Libby Handy. Illustrations copyright © 1982 by Jack Newnham. Reprinted by permission of Ashton Scholastic Limited NZ. *The Poem*: By Marjorie Weinman Sharmat, Pictures by Lillian Hoban. Original title SOPHIE AND GUSSIE. Reprinted with permission of Macmillan Publishing Co., Inc. from SOPHIE AND GUSSIE by Marjorie Weinman Sharmat and Lillian Hoban. Copyright © 1973 by Marjorie Weinman Sharmat. Copyright © 1973 by Lillian Hoban. *Ralph's Dog*: From CONVERSATIONS WITH MARIA by J. McLeod. Reprinted by permission of Alive Press Ltd. (Guelph), 1974. *Split Pea Soup*: From GEORGE AND MARTHA by James Marshall. Copyright © 1972 by James Marshall. Reprinted by permission of Houghton Mifflin Company. *The Corner*: By Arnold Lobel (text and specified illustrations) from FROG AND TOAD ALL YEAR by Arnold Lobel. Copyright © 1976 by Arnold Lobel. By permission of Harper & Row, Publishers, Inc. *You'll Sing a Song and I'll Sing a Song*: Words by Ella Jenkins from her record album (Folkways Records FC7664—Ellbern Publishing Company, 1844 North Mohawk Street, Chicago, Illinois 60614, USA.) *My Friend Jacob*: By Lucille Clifton, illustrated by Thomas DiGrazia. Text copyright © 1980 by Lucille Clifton. Illustrations copyright © 1980 by Thomas DiGrazia, Reprinted by permission of the publisher, E.P. Dutton, Inc. *Kate's Secret Riddle Book*: From KATE'S SECRET RIDDLE BOOK by Sid Fleischman. Text copyright © 1977 by Albert S. Fleischman. Used by permissions of Franklin Watts, Inc. *July*: From SUNFLAKES AND SHOWSHINE by Fran Newman and Claudette Boulanger. Reprinted by permission of Scholastic-TAB Publications. *Under the Shade of the Mulberry Tree*: Reprinted by permission of The Julian Bach Literary Agency. Copyright © 1979 by Demi Hitz. *August Afternoon*: Marion Edey and Dorothy Grider, "August Afternoon," in OPEN THE DOOR. Copyright 1949 Marion Edey and Dorothy Grider. Reprinted with the permission of Charles Scribner's Sons. *Alligator's Sunday Suit*: Adapted by permission of Philomel Books, a division of The Putman Publishing Group, from BO RABBIT SMART FOR TRUE by Priscilla Jaquith. Text copyright © 1981 by Priscilla Jaquith, illustrations copyright © 1981 by Ed Young. *Rhymes Without Reason*: "Here I am, little jumping Joan", "The grand old Duke of York". "Hector Protector was dressed all in green", "Higglety, pigglety, pop!" and "Diddle, diddle, dumpling..." from GRANFA' GRIG HAD A PIG: AND OTHER RHYMES WITHOUT REASON FROM MOTHER GOOSE, compiled and illustrated by Wallace Tripp. Illustrations Copyright © 1976 by Wallace Tripp. By permission of Little, Brown and Company. *Anansi*: Words by Bert Simpson. © Copyright 1979 Homeland Publishing. Used by permission. From the album "The Corner Grocery Store" by Raffi.

Every reasonable effort has been made to trace the owners of copyrighted material and to make due acknowledgement. Any errors or omissions drawn to our attention will be gladly rectified in future editions.

Table of Contents

Help!

by
Jack Prelutsky

Can anybody tell me, please,
a bit about the thing
with seven legs and furry knees,
four noses and a wing?

Oh what has prickles on its chin,
what's yellow, green, and blue,
and what has soft and slimy skin?
Oh tell me, tell me, do.

And tell me, what has polka dots
on every other ear,
what ties its tail in twenty knots,
what weeps a purple tear?

Oh what is growling long and low
and please, has it been fed?
I think I'd really better know...
it's sitting on my head.

I Can Lick 30 Tigers Today!

by
Dr. Seuss

I can lick
thirty tigers today!

Well...
Maybe twenty-nine.
You!
Down there!
With the curly hair.
Will you please step out of the line.

I can lick
twenty-nine tigers today...

Well...
That's sort of
A mean thing to do.
I'll cut down my list.
First group is dismissed.
I'll beat up the next twenty-two.

I can lick
Twenty-two tigers today...

Well...
Maybe I'll lick thirteen.
You! In the front row.
You're excused! You may go.
Your fingernails aren't very clean.

I can lick
Thirteen tigers today...

Well . . . .

Quite a few of you
seem underweight.
It's not fair, after all,
To lick tigers so small.
I think that I'll only lick eight.

I can lick
Eight big tigers today...

Well...
You look sort of sleepy to me.
Some of you chaps
Should go home and take naps.
I only intend to lick three.

I can lick
Three big tigers today...

Well...
It's frightfully hot
In the sun.
You two, I'm afraid,
Should lie down in the shade.
You're safe.
I shall only lick one.

I can lick
One mighty tiger today...

But...
You know, I have sort of a hunch
That noontime is near.
You just wait for me here.
I'll beat you up right after lunch.

Who to Pet
and Who Not to

by
X.J. Kennedy

Go pet a kitten, pet a dog,
Go pet a worm for practice,
But don't go pet a porcupine—
You want to be a cactus?

Mine Will, Said John

by
Helen V. Griffith

John and his parents were at the pet shop.
They were buying a pet for John.

"I would like a puppy," said John.

"Puppies are noisy," said his mother.
"That is why we are buying you this nice gerbil."

"Gerbils are noisy, too," said John.
"They cry at night."

"Gerbils don't make any noise at all," his father said.

"Mine will," said John.

That night John put the gerbil in a box by his bed.
He climbed into bed and turned off the light.
The gerbil began to whimper.
Then the gerbil began to yelp. It yelped and yelped.

John's parents came into the room.

"Did we hear something?" asked John's mother.

"The gerbil," said John.

They all looked at the gerbil.
It was curled up and sound asleep.

"It keeps me awake," said John.

John's parents looked at John.
Then they looked at each other.

The next day they took the gerbil back
to the pet shop.

"It makes too much noise," John said.

"Gerbils don't make noise," said the pet shop owner.

"Mine did," said John.

They exchanged the gerbil for a chameleon.

"A chameleon will be nice and quiet,"
said John's mother.

"Chameleons glow in the dark," said John.
"They turn blue and pink and orange and purple."

"Chameleons turn green and brown, that's all,"
said John's father. "They don't glow in the dark."

"Mine will," said John.

That night John put the chameleon in a box by his bed.
He climbed into bed and turned off the light.
The chameleon began to glow.
It turned blue and pink and orange and purple.
The whole room began to glow.
John put the chameleon under his blanket,
but the colours glowed through it —
purple and orange and pink and blue.

John's parents came into the room.

"Did we see something?" asked John's father.

"The chameleon," said John.

They all looked at the chameleon.
It was lying on its back sound asleep.

"It keeps me awake," said John.

John's parents looked at John.
Then they looked at each other.

At the pet shop the next day John said,
"My chameleon glowed in the dark."

"Chameleons don't glow in the dark,"
said the pet shop owner.

"Mine did," said John.

"I think we will exchange the chameleon for a frog," said John's mother. "Would you like a pet frog, John?"

"Frogs chew on furniture," said John.
"They chew all night long."

"Frogs don't have teeth," said John's father.
"They can't chew anything."

"Mine will," said John.

John's parents looked at each other.
Then they looked at John.

"Okay, John," said his father. "You win.
Which one do you want?"

"This one," said John. "He won't cry at night
and he won't glow in the dark
and he won't chew furniture. He will always mind me,
and he will love me better than anything."

"Now, John," said his mother,
"I don't think any puppy can be that good."

"Mine will," said John.

And it was.

Like a Giant in a Towel

by
Dennis Lee

When the wind is blowing hard
Like a giant in the yard,
  I'm glad my bed is warm;
  I'm glad my bed is warm.

When the rain begins to rain
Like a giant with a pain,
  I'm glad my bed is warm;
  I'm glad my bed is warm.

When the snowstorm starts to howl
Like a giant in a towel,
  I'm glad my bed is warm;
  I'm glad my bed is warm.

And when the giants realize
That no one's scared of their disguise,
They go to bed and close their eyes—
  They're glad their beds are warm;
  They're glad their beds are warm.

The Hungry Thing

by
Jan Slepian and Ann Seidler

One morning a Hungry Thing came to town.
He sat on his tail. He pointed to a sign around his neck
that said **Feed Me**. The townspeople gathered around
to see the Hungry Thing.

"What would you like to eat?" asked the townspeople.

"Shmancakes," answered the Hungry Thing.

"Shmancakes!" cried the townspeople.
"How do you eat them? What can they be?"

"Why, dear me," said a Wiseman,
"shmancakes, that's plain,
Are a small kind of chicken
that falls with the rain."

"Of course," said a Cook,
"shmancakes, I've read,
Are better to eat
when you stand on your head."

"I think," said a little boy, "you're all very silly.
Shmancakes...sound like...
Fancakes...sound like...
Pancakes to me."

So the townspeople gave the Hungry Thing some.
The Hungry Thing ate them all up.
Then the Hungry Thing pointed to his sign
that said **Feed Me**.

"What would you like to eat?" asked the townspeople.

"Tickles," answered the Hungry Thing.

"Tickles!" cried the townspeople.
"How do you eat them? What can they be?"

"Why, dear me," said the Wiseman.
"Tickles, you know,
Are curly tailed hot dogs
that grow in a row."

"Of course," said the Cook,
"tickles taste yummy,
And you giggle and laugh
with ten in your tummy!"

"I think," said the little boy, "it's all very clear.
Tickles...sound like...
Sickels...sound like...
Pickles to me."

And they gave the Hungry Thing some.
The Hungry Thing ate them all up.

"He's underfed.
Have some bread,"
Said a lady
Dressed in red.

"It seems to me
He'd like some tea,"
Said a fellow
Up a tree.

"A bit of rice
Might be nice,"
Said a baby,
Sucking ice.

The Hungry Thing just shook his head
and pointed to his sign that said **Feed Me**.
The townspeople tried again.

"What would you like to eat?" asked the townspeople.

"Feetloaf," answered the Hungry Thing.

"Feetloaf!" cried the townspeople. "How do you eat it?
What can it be?"

"Why, dear me," said the Wiseman.
"Feetloaf, let's see...
It's a kind of shoe pudding
that grows in a tree."

"Of course," said the Cook,
"feetloaf tastes sweet,
And it's eaten by kings
when they dine in bare feet."

"I think," said the little boy, "you all ought to know.
Feetloaf...sounds like...
Beetloaf...sounds like...
Meatloaf to me."

So the townspeople gave the Hungry Thing some.
The Hungry Thing ate it all up. He again pointed
to his sign that said **Feed Me**.

"What would you like this time?"
asked the townspeople.

"Hookies," answered the Hungry Thing.

"Hookies!" cried the townspeople.
"How do you eat them? What can they be?"

"Hookies," said the Wiseman,
"are known in far lands
As a special spaghetti
to eat holding hands."

"Hookies," said the Cook,
"are a party dish
To serve to a guest
if he isn't a fish."

"I think," said the little boy, "that it's all very simple.
Hookies...sound like...
Lookies...sound like...
Cookies to me."

The townspeople gave the Hungry Thing some.
And he ate them all up. Then he got to his feet.
He smiled. He patted his mouth on a line of laundry.
He turned around three times.

"Is it true
He's all through?"
Asked a lady
Dressed in blue.

"Let's all try
To say goodbye,"
Said a man
With a can.

"Come again!"
Said some men.

But the Hungry Thing just sat down again.
And he pointed to his sign that said **Feed Me**.

"What do you want to eat?" asked the townspeople.

"Gollipops," said the Hungry Thing.

"Gollipops!" cried the townspeople.
"How do you eat them? What can they be?"

"Oh, dear me!" said the Wiseman.
"Gollipops are new.
They are cereal shaped like toys.
And sugar-coated, too!"

"Children," said the Cook,
"buy them by the dozens
And trade off the box tops
with classmates and cousins."

"I think," said the boy, "you all ought to hear.
Gollipops...sound like...
Dollipops...sound like...
Lollipops to me."

So the townspeople gave the Hungry Thing some.
The Hungry Thing ate them all up. And he pointed
to his sign again.

"Oh please!" said the people.
"We've been here all day.
Isn't there a quicker way?"

"I think," said the boy, "that there is."

"Have some noodles?" the little boy asked
the Hungry Thing.

The Hungry Thing shook his head.

"Oh, excuse me, I meant to say...foodles."

The Hungry Thing smiled and ate them all up.

"Just look!"
Said the Cook.

"Let's all try!"
Was the cry.

So they all got busy.

"Have some smello."
They gave him some Jello.

"Have some thread."
They gave him some bread.

"Have a fanana."
They gave him a banana.

The Hungry Thing ate and ate. He looked very full.
"Is there anything more we can give you?"
the townspeople wanted to know.

The Hungry Thing politely covered a hiccup.
He thought for a while. Then...

"Boop with a smacker," he said.

"Boop with a smacker? Boop with a smacker?
What is that?" the townspeople asked.

The boy whispered to the Wiseman.
The Wiseman whispered to the Cook.
And the Cook gave the Hungry Thing...
Soup with a cracker.

The Hungry Thing ate them all up. He smiled.
He got to his feet. He wiped his mouth
on the Cook's hat. Just as he left he turned
his sign around. In big letters it said THANK YOU!

Dinosaur Time

by
Peggy Parish

Long, long ago
the world was different.
More land was under water.
It was warm all the time.
And dinosaurs
were everywhere....

There were big dinosaurs.
There were small ones.
There were fast dinosaurs,
and slow ones.
Some dinosaurs ate meat.
Some ate plants.

BRONTOSAURUS

This is how you say it—
bron-tuh-SAW-russ.

This dinosaur
was a giant.
But its mouth was tiny.
It ate plants.
It ate, and ate, and ate
to fill up its big body.

Its name is **Brontosaurus**.

ANATOSAURUS

This is how you say it—
an-at-oh-SAW-russ.

This dinosaur
was called a "duckbill."
It had a beak like a duck.
Its beak had no teeth.
But its mouth did.
There were
hundreds of teeth in it!
Sometimes a tooth broke.
But that did not matter.
It could grow a new one.

Its name is **Anatosaurus**.

BRACHIOSAURUS

This is how you say it—
brack-ee-oh-SAW-russ.

This dinosaur was fat.
It was too fat
to run from enemies.
That is why it stayed in the water.
It was safe there,
and food was close by.
It ate plants.

Its name is **Brachiosaurus**.

TYRANNOSAURUS

This is how you say it—
tih-ran-uh-SAW-russ.

This dinosaur
was the biggest meat-eater.
Its jaws were huge.
Its teeth were fifteen centimetres long.
It ate other dinosaurs.

Its name is **Tyrannosaurus.**

Dinosaurs lived everywhere
for a long time.
Then they died.
Nobody knows why.
But once it was their world.
It was dinosaur time.

Company

by
Bobbi Katz

I'm fixing a lunch for a dinosaur.
Who knows when one might come by?
I'm pulling up all the weeds I can find.
I'm piling them high as the sky.
I'm fixing a lunch for a dinosaur.
I hope he will stop by soon.
Maybe he'll just walk down my street
And stop for lunch at noon.

48

There Is a Place
by
Arnold Adoff

There is a place
on the couch
    for
      grandma
and
a place on
      grandma
for me
    in front
    of
    the
      fire
        and pop
        ping
        corn

Little Bear Goes to the Moon

by
Else Holmelund Minarik

"I have a new space helmet. I am going to the moon," said Little Bear to Mother Bear.

"How?" asked Mother Bear.

"I'm going to fly to the moon," said Little Bear.

"Fly!" said Mother Bear. "You can't fly."

"Birds fly," said Little Bear.

"Oh, yes," said Mother Bear. "Birds fly,
but they don't fly to the moon.
And you are not a bird."

"Maybe some birds fly to the moon, I don't know.
And maybe I can fly like a bird," said Little Bear.

"And maybe," said Mother Bear,
"you are a little fat bear cub with no wings
and no feathers. Maybe if you jump up
you will come down very fast, with a big plop."

"Maybe," said Little Bear. "But I'm going now.
Just look for me up in the sky."

"Be back for lunch," said Mother.

Little Bear thought. I will jump from a good high spot,
far up into the sky, and fly up, up, up. I will be going
too fast to look at things, so I will shut my eyes.

Little Bear climbed to the top of a little hill,
and climbed to the top of a little tree,
a very little tree on the little hill,
and shut his eyes and jumped.
Down, down he came with a big plop,
and down the hill he tumbled.
Then he sat up and looked around.

"My, my," he said. "Here I am on the moon.
The moon looks just like the Earth.
Well, well," said Little Bear.
"The trees here look just like our trees.
The birds look just like our birds.
And look at this," he said.
"Here is a house that looks just like my house.
I'll go in and see what kind of bears live here."

"Look at that," said Little Bear.
"Something to eat is on the table.
It looks like a good lunch for a little bear."

Mother Bear came in and said,
"But who is this?
Are you a bear from Earth?"

"Oh, yes, I am," said Little Bear.
"I climbed a little hill,
and jumped from a little tree,
and flew here, just like the birds."

"Well," said Mother Bear.
"My little bear did the same thing.
He put on his space helmet and flew to Earth.
So I guess you can have his lunch."

Little Bear put his arms around Mother Bear.
He said, "Mother Bear, stop fooling.
You are my Mother Bear
and I am your Little Bear,
and we are on Earth, and you know it.
Now may I eat my lunch?"

"Yes," said Mother Bear,
"and then you will have your nap.
For you are my little bear,
and I know it."

A Teeny Weeny Girl

by
David Booth and Meguido Zola

A teeny weeny girl
lived on a teeny weeny mountain
in a teeny weeny house
by a teeny weeny lake
with her teeny weeny mother
and her teeny weeny father
but no one to play with.

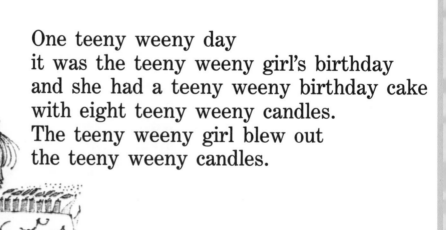

One teeny weeny day
it was the teeny weeny girl's birthday
and she had a teeny weeny birthday cake
with eight teeny weeny candles.
The teeny weeny girl blew out
the teeny weeny candles.

She ate the teeny weeny birthday cake
with her teeny weeny father
and her teeny weeny mother
and saw her teeny weeny present
wrapped in teeny weeny paper
with a teeny weeny bow.

Inside the teeny weeny box
was a teeny weeny puppy
wagging his teeny weeny tail
and giving a teeny weeny bark
with a teeny weeny note
in his teeny weeny mouth
that said:
Here is a teeny weeny dog
for a teeny weeny girl!

Daniel's Duck

by
Clyde Robert Bulla

Chapter 1

Jeff and Daniel were brothers.
They lived in a cabin on a mountain.

Jeff had a good knife.
He could carve with it.
He could carve things out of wood.
He made a dish.
He made a cup and a spoon.
His mother and father were proud.

"Some day," they said, "you may be
as good as Henry Pettigrew."

Henry Pettigrew lived in the valley.
They had never seen him,
but they had seen his work.
He was a wood-carver.
Some said he was the best wood-carver
they had ever known.

Henry Pettigrew carved animals.
His birds looked as if they could fly.
His horses looked as if they could run.
All his animals looked real.
Jeff and his brother Daniel
had seen some of them in town.

"I want to carve an animal," said Jeff.
"I want to carve a deer or a turkey
or a bear like Henry Pettigrew's.
But animals are hard to do."

"I want to carve an animal, too," said Daniel.

"You're not old enough," said Jeff.

"Yes, I am," said Daniel. "I could carve one
if I had a good knife and some wood."

"It takes more than a good knife and some wood,"
said Jeff.

"What does it take?" asked Daniel.

"You have to know how," said Jeff.
"It's hard to carve an animal."

"I know how," said Daniel.

"Let's see if you do," said his father.
He gave Daniel a knife like Jeff's.
He gave him a block of wood.

It was winter.
The nights were long.

"This is a good time to sit by the fire
and carve," said Jeff.
"I'm going to make something
for the spring fair."

Every spring there was a fair in the valley.
It was time for people to meet after the long winter.
It was a time to show things that they had made.
Sometimes they sold what they had made.
Sometimes they traded with one another.

Father knew how to make moccasins.
On winter nights he made moccasins
to take to the fair.

Mother cut pieces of cloth. She sewed them together
to make a quilt.

"This will be a warm quilt for somebody's bed,"
she said. "I'll take it to the fair."

"I'm going to make a box for the fair," said Jeff.
"I'm going to carve little moons on the lid."

He said to his brother, "You haven't done anything
with your block of wood. What are you going to make?"

"I have to think," said Daniel.

Days went by.

Then Daniel began to carve.

"What are you making?" asked Jeff.

"You'll see," said Daniel.

One night Jeff looked at what Daniel was carving. He saw a neck and a head. He saw a wing.

"Now I see," he said. "It's a bird."

"It's a duck," said Daniel.

"You're not doing it right," said Jeff. "Its head is on backward."

"I want it that way," said Daniel. "My duck is looking back."

"That's no way to do it," said Jeff.

Father said, "Let him do it his way."

Chapter 2

Spring came.

It was time for the fair.
Mother had made her quilt.
Father had made three pairs of moccasins.

Jeff's box was done.
"It took a long time," he said.

"My duck took a long time, too,"
said Daniel.

"Are you sure you want to take it
to the fair?" asked Jeff.

"Yes," said Daniel.

They went down the mountain in a wagon.
Father drove the horses.
They drove into town.
There were people everywhere.
Everyone had come to the fair.

Father took the quilt and the moccasins.
He took Jeff's box and Daniel's duck.
He left them at the hall.

The hall was a long house
in the middle of town.
"This is where the show will be,"
said Father. "People are getting it ready now."

They walked down the street.
They saw the river.
They talked with friends.

Father said, "The hall is open."

They went to the show.
There were pictures that people had made.
There were quilts and rugs and baskets.
There were dolls. There were jams and jellies.

"Where are the wood carvings?" asked Daniel.

"Over here," said Jeff.

They went to the end of the hall.
The carvings were there on tables.
On a small table was a carved deer.
It was so beautiful that people were quiet
when they looked at it.
Everyone knew it had been done
by Henry Pettigrew.

On a big table were the carvings
that others had done.

"I see my box," said Jeff.

"I see my duck," said Daniel.

Many people were looking at the carvings.
They were laughing.

"What are they laughing at?" asked Daniel.

Jeff didn't answer.

Someone said, "Look at the duck!"

Someone else said, "That duck is so funny!"

More people came to look.
More people were laughing.

Now Daniel knew.

They were laughing at his duck.
He wanted to go away.
He wanted to hide.

Then he was angry.
He went to the table.
He picked up his duck
and ran with it.
He ran out of the hall.

Someone was running after him.
Daniel ran faster.
He came to the river.
He started to throw the duck
as far as he could.
But he could not throw it.

A man had hold of his arm.
The man asked, "What are you doing
with that duck?"

"I'm going to throw it in the river!"
said Daniel.

"You can't do that," said the man.

"I can if I want to," said Daniel.
"It's mine."

"Did you make it?" asked the man.

"Yes," said Daniel.

"Why were you going to throw it away?"
asked the man.

"They all laughed at it," said Daniel.

"Listen to me," said the man.
"There are different ways of laughing.
The people liked your duck.
They laughed because they liked it."

"No. It's ugly," said Daniel.

"It isn't ugly. It's a good duck.
It made me feel happy.
That's why I laughed."

The man was not laughing now.

"You're hot and tired," he said.
"Come and rest in the shade."

They sat under a tree.

"Would you sell your duck?"
asked the man.

"Who would buy it?"
asked Daniel.

"I might think of someone,"
said the man.

A boy and girl came up to them.

"How are you, Mr. Pettigrew?" they asked.

"I'm fine," said the man.
The boy and girl went on.

Daniel said, "You're Henry Pettigrew!"

"Yes," said the man. "I'm a wood-carver, too."

"I know that," said Daniel.

He was holding his duck.
He looked down at it.
It wasn't ugly.
It was a good duck.
Henry Pettigrew had said so,
and he knew.

"I saw your deer," said Daniel.

"I made it last winter," said the man.
"I've made lots of things.
My house is full of them."

Daniel said, "I wish—" and then he stopped.

"What do you wish?" asked the man.

"I wish I could see the things
you've made," said Daniel.

"I'll show them to you," said the man.
"Maybe today, after the fair."
"Shall we go back to the fair now?"

"Yes," said Daniel.

They got up.
The man was looking at the duck.

"Will you sell it to me?" he asked.

"No," said Daniel.

He held the duck a little longer.

Then he gave it to Henry Pettigrew.

The Gentle Giant

by
Dennis Lee

Every night
At twelve o'clock
The gentle giant
Takes a walk;
With a cry cried high
And a call called low,
the gentle giant
Walks below.

And as he walks,
He cries, he calls:

"Bad men, boogie men,
Bully men, shoo!
No one in the neighbourhood
Is scared of you.
The children are asleep,
And the parents are too:
Bad men, boogie men,
Bully men, shoo!"

Reggie Alone!

by
Shirley Benton Kerr

Reggie squirmed in his seat. It was hard to listen to his teacher. All he could think of was the fact that he had to go home to an empty house at noon. He felt under his shirt for his brand new key. It was still there.

"You're old enough now," his mother had told him, "to come in at noon and get your lunch out of the refrigerator."

"What if you forget to leave it?" Reggie asked.

"I won't forget to leave it," his mother promised.

This morning before she left for work
she had pointed out the plate to him on the top shelf
of the refrigerator. On it were a sandwich,
some celery sticks, some cookies and an apple.

"You can pour yourself a glass of milk," she said.

"What if I spill it?" Reggie asked.

"I'm sure you won't spill it," his mother said firmly,
"but if you do, then you'll have to wipe it up."

Reggie knew that Mom's new job was important to her
so he knew he had to try.

He sighed as the hands on the classroom clock
moved steadily on to twelve o'clock.
When the lunch bell rang he slowly made his way
to his coat and boots. Slowly he put them on.

It was funny. He used to envy kids who had
their own keys. He thought it would be great
to be able to go home and let himself in
with his own key. Now he wasn't so sure.

As he walked up the path to his house
he thought the house looked silent and lonely.
He pulled his new key out and opened the door.
He went in and listened. Not a sound could he hear.
He quickly turned on the radio. That was better.
Then he went to the refrigerator and took out
his lunch. He put it on the table
and carefully poured himself a glass of milk.
When he picked up his sandwich
there was a piece of paper underneath.

"Dear Reggie," it said. "I knew you could do it.
I'm proud of you. I hope you have a good day.
See you tonight. Love, Mom."

"Thank you, Mom," Reggie whispered. He tucked
into his lunch, then rinsed his glass and plate
in the sink. He read a book until it was time
to go back to school.

As he left the house he knew he wouldn't mind
coming home alone any more.
He still didn't like it really, but Mom had to work
and he didn't want her to worry about him.

The Incredible Dog

by
Melanie Zola

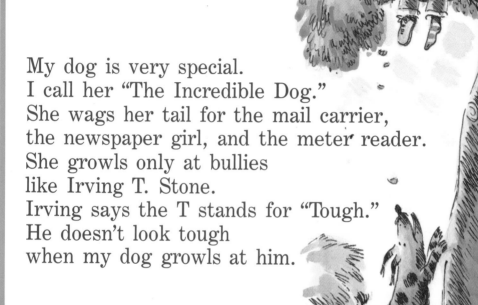

My dog is very special.
I call her "The Incredible Dog."
She wags her tail for the mail carrier,
the newspaper girl, and the meter reader.
She growls only at bullies
like Irving T. Stone.
Irving says the T stands for "Tough."
He doesn't look tough
when my dog growls at him.

My dog doesn't chase every car,
just cars that are speeding.
They deserve it.

After a bubble-bath,
my dog shakes her fur
and gets me wet too.

She can jump a two-metre fence
with a single leap.
I never lose a ball when my dog's around.

My dog knows all the tricks.
Say "shake-a-paw"
and you will have one in your hand.
Say "stay" and she almost goes
to sleep right there on the spot.

If I have yucky things I know I can't eat,
I just shuffle my feet.
My dog gets the message.
She is ready to save me from bread crusts and carrots.
She is faster than
the eye can see.

My dog never lets me down.
She is always ready to cuddle against me
and let me scratch her neck.

It doesn't matter who is mad at me,
or how badly I feel.
My dog is there.
Right there beside me.
Right there in my heart!

Barn Owl

by
Phyllis Flower

High in the corner of the barn,
the barn owl sits and waits.
She has been sitting on her eggs
for nearly a month.

Sometimes during the day
her mate sits beside her.
When she is hungry,
he brings her food.

At last she feels something move
beneath her.
She stands up
and looks down at her eggs.
They are white and oval,
smaller than hens' eggs.

Last night there were five.
But now there are four.
Next to them
she sees a small white mound.
The barn owl bobs her head
up and down.
She looks at her new baby.

He has tiny white feathers called *down*.
They are wet now.
But they will dry soon
and become fluffy.
His face is heart-shaped
like his mother's.
His eyes are closed.

His beak is curved.
On the end of his beak
is a special tooth, an *egg* tooth.
The owlet used it
to break open his shell.
It will fall off soon,
for he no longer needs it.
His ears are openings in his head,
hidden under feathers.

He has four strong toes on each foot.
On the end of each toe
is a sharp hook.
It is called a *talon*.
Someday he will use his talons
for hunting.
One talon has a very rough edge.
He will use it
to comb his feathers.

Now the owlet is tired.
Breaking open his shell
was hard work.
He needs to rest.
So he cuddles
under his mother's feathers
and sleeps.

When he wakes up,
he is hungry.
He is ready for the food
his father brings him.
The owlet has a big appetite.
He spends his time
sleeping and eating.

In two days another egg hatches.
The owlet has a brother.

Soon all the eggs have hatched.

When he is about a week old,
the owlet's eyes open.
They are large and round
and dark brown.
He can see well at night with them.
But he can see only straight ahead.
He cannot move his eyes
up or down.
He cannot move them
from side to side.

He has to turn his whole head
to look to the side.
He can turn his head
all the way around
and look behind him.

Now he sees his parents
for the first time.
His mother is a little larger
than his father.
Each has a white face and chest.

Now the owlet is covered
with short, woolly feathers.

The five baby owls
are growing larger.
And they need more food.
The mother owl goes
with her mate
to find enough food.

They hunt at night
for rats and mice, small birds,
moths and other insects.
They fly silently.
They can hear a mouse
running over the ground.
They can see a beetle
crawling out from under a rock.

When they find a mouse or rat,
they swoop down on it.
They kill it with their sharp talons.

Then they carry it to the nest.

The babies are waiting for them
with open mouths.

They are always hungry.

Owl Questions

by
David Booth

Why do you hoot, Owl?
What do you see?
What do you want, Owl,
Up in your tree?

What do you spy, Owl,
Far down below?
Turning your head, Owl,
What do you know?

Why hunt at night, Owl?
Moon's in the sky.
Daybreak will come, Owl,
Where will you fly?

Where is your child, Owl?
I see the dawn!
Why are you sad, Owl?
Owlet has gone.

Too Much Noise

by
Ann McGovern

A long time ago there was an old man.
His name was Peter, and he lived in an old, old house.

The bed creaked. The floor squeaked.
Outside, the wind blew the leaves through the trees.
The leaves fell on the roof. *Swish. Swish.*
The tea kettle whistled. *Hiss. Hiss.*

"Too noisy," said Peter.

Peter went to see the wise man of the village.

"What can I do?" Peter asked the wise man.
"My house makes too much noise.
My bed creaks.
My floor squeaks.
The wind blows the leaves through the trees.
The leaves fall on the roof. *Swish. Swish.*
My tea kettle whistles. *Hiss. Hiss.*"

"I can help you," the wise man said.
"I know what you can do."

"What?" said Peter.

"Get a cow," said the wise man.

"What good is a cow?" said Peter.
But Peter got a cow anyhow.

The cow said, "Moo. MOO."
The bed creaked.
The floor squeaked.
The leaves fell on the roof. *Swish. Swish.*
The tea kettle whistled. *Hiss. Hiss.*

"Too noisy," said Peter.
And he went back to the wise man.

"Get a donkey," said the wise man.

"What good is a donkey?" said Peter.
But Peter got a donkey anyhow.

The donkey said, "HEE-Haw."
The cow said, "Moo. MOO."
The bed creaked.
The floor squeaked.
The leaves fell on the roof. *Swish. Swish.*
The tea kettle whistled. *Hiss. Hiss.*

"Still too noisy," said Peter.
And he went back to the wise man.

"Get a sheep," said the wise man.

"What good is a sheep?" said Peter.
But Peter got a sheep anyhow.

The sheep said, "Baa. Baa."
The donkey said, "HEE-Haw."
The cow said, "Moo. MOO."
The bed creaked.
The floor squeaked.
The leaves fell on the roof. *Swish. Swish.*
The tea kettle whistled. *Hiss. Hiss.*

"Too noisy," said Peter.
And he went back to the wise man.

"Get a hen," said the wise man.

"What good is a hen?" said Peter.
But Peter got a hen anyhow.

The hen said, "Cluck. Cluck."
The sheep said, "Baa. Baa."
The donkey said, "HEE-Haw."
The cow said, "Moo. MOO."
The bed creaked.
The floor squeaked.
The leaves fell on the roof. *Swish. Swish.*
The tea kettle whistled. *Hiss. Hiss.*

"Too noisy," said Peter.
And back he went to the wise man.

"Get a dog," the wise man said.
"And get a cat too."

"What good is a dog?" said Peter. "Or a cat?"
But Peter got a dog and a cat anyhow.

The dog said, "Woof. Woof."
The cat said, "Mee-ow. Mee-ow."
The hen said, "Cluck. Cluck."
The sheep said, "Baa. Baa."
The donkey said, "HEE-Haw."
The cow said, "Moo. MOO."
The bed creaked.
The floor squeaked.
The leaves fell on the roof. *Swish. Swish.*
The tea kettle whistled. *Hiss. Hiss.*

Now Peter was angry.
He went to the wise man.

"I told you my house was too noisy," he said.
"I told you my bed creaks.
My floor squeaks.
The leaves fall on the roof. *Swish. Swish.*
The tea kettle whistles. *Hiss. Hiss.*
You told me to get a cow.
All day the cow says, 'Moo. MOO.'
You told me to get a donkey.
All day the donkey says, 'HEE-Haw.'
You told me to get a sheep.
All day the sheep says, 'Baa. Baa.'
You told me to get a hen.
All day the hen says, 'Cluck. Cluck.'
You told me to get a dog.
And a cat.
All day the dog says, 'Woof. Woof.'
All day the cat says, 'Mee-ow. Mee-ow.'
I am going crazy," said Peter.

The wise man said, "Do what I tell you.
Let the cow go.
Let the donkey go.
Let the sheep go.
Let the hen go.
Let the dog go.
Let the cat go."

So Peter let the cow go.
He let the donkey go.
He let the sheep go.
He let the hen go.
He let the dog go.
He let the cat go.

Now no cow said, "Moo. MOO."
No donkey said, "HEE-Haw."
No sheep said, "Baa. Baa."
No hen said, "Cluck. Cluck."
No dog said, "Woof. Woof."
No cat said, "Mee-ow. Mee-ow."

The bed creaked.

"Ah," said Peter. "What a quiet noise."

The floor squeaked.

"Oh," said Peter. "What a quiet noise."

Outside the leaves fell on the roof. *Swish. Swish.*
Inside the tea kettle whistled. *Hiss. Hiss.*

"Ah. Oh," said Peter. "How quiet my house is."

And Peter got into his bed and went to sleep and dreamed a very

quiet

dream.

Before I Count Fifteen

by
Michael Rosen

115

The Real Princess

Retold by David Booth

Once upon a time,
a Prince decided he wanted to marry a Princess.
Not just any Princess.
A real Princess.
He travelled around the world to find one.
There were plenty of Princesses.
But how could the Prince tell
if they were real Princesses?
At last he came home again.
He was very sad
because he wanted to marry a real Princess.

One night there was a terrible storm.
The rain poured down.
The thunder roared.
The lightning flashed.

Suddenly, somebody knocked
at the town gate.
The old King opened it.
A Princess stood outside in the rain.
Her dress was wet.
Her hair was wet.
Her shoes were wet.
But she said, "I am a real Princess."

The Queen decided to test the Princess.
Maybe she was a real Princess.
Maybe she was not a real Princess.

The old Queen went into the bedroom.
She took everything off the bed.
She laid a pea on the spring.
Then she piled twenty mattresses on top of the pea.
Then she piled twenty feather beds
on top of the mattresses.

That night, the Princess went to sleep
on the strange bed.

In the morning, the family asked her
how she had slept.

"Oh, very badly!" said the Princess.
"I hardly closed my eyes all night!
I seemed to be lying on some hard thing.
My whole body is black and blue this morning.
I feel terrible!"

The old King and Queen saw at once
that she must be a real Princess.
She had felt the pea
through twenty mattresses and twenty feather beds.
Nobody but a real Princess
could have such delicate skin.

So the Prince married the Princess.
He was sure that she was a real Princess.

The pea was put into the museum.
You may still see it there,
if no one has stolen it.

Porridge for Everyone

Retold by Jack Booth

Dear Anna,

Thank you for your letter about summer camp.
Cooking outside is so much fun!
It reminds me of meals long ago.
I loved to eat porridge
when I was a little girl.
I filled my beautiful blue bowl
with three big spoons of porridge.
Then I put raisins in the bowl.
Then I put on three spoons of brown sugar.
I covered everything
with three big splashes of cream.
How delicious!
I am making myself hungry.

Here is a little story for you.
It is all about porridge.
I hope you enjoy it
as much as I enjoyed my porridge
long, long ago.

Once upon a time there was a little girl
who was very poor.
She lived with her mother in a small village.
They were so poor that many nights
they had to go to bed hungry.
At last, there was nothing left to eat.

One day the girl went into the woods
to find some nuts or berries.
There, she met an old woman.
The poor girl told her story to the old woman.
The woman gave the girl a little cooking pot.
She told the girl to put the pot on the stove and say,
"Cook, little pot, cook!"
She said the pot would bubble and boil
and cook porridge for the girl and her mother.
The pot would stop cooking if the girl said,
"Stop, little pot, stop!"

And that is what happened.
The girl took the pot home to her mother.
The two could eat all the porridge they wanted.
They were never hungry any more.

One day the girl went away for a few hours.
The hungry mother said, "Cook, little pot, cook."

Soon, a wonderful smell filled the kitchen.
The pot began to cook.
Soon the mother was eating a big bowl
of sweet porridge.
When she was full, she wanted to stop the pot.
But she had forgotten the words!

So, the little pot kept on cooking.
It cooked and cooked and cooked.
It cooked some more,
until it ran all over the stove.
It cooked and cooked
until the house was full of porridge.
It cooked and cooked
until the porridge ran out of the windows.
It cooked and cooked
until the porridge ran into the street,
and into the houses along the way.

The people ran from their houses.
They ran from the porridge.
The porridge bubbled and boiled
until it filled the whole village.
It ran over the farms.
No one knew what to do.

At last the little girl returned.
She saw what had happened and said,
"Stop, little pot, stop!"
The pot stopped cooking at once.
But there was only one way
the villagers could get back
to their houses.
They had to eat their way
through the porridge!

Well, that is my porridge story.
Write again soon, Anna.
Happy Porridge Time!

Love,

Grandma

What Did You Put in Your Pocket?

by
Beatrice Schenk de Regniers

What did you put in your pocket
What did you put in your pocket
   in your pockety pockety pocket
Early Monday morning?

I put in some chocolate pudding
I put in some chocolate pudding
   slushy glushy pudding
Early Monday morning.

   SLUSHY GLUSHY PUDDING!

What did you put in your pocket
What did you put in your pocket
  in your pockety pockety pocket
Early Tuesday morning?

I put in some ice-cold water
I put in some ice-cold water
  nicy icy water
Early Tuesday morning.

SLUSHY GLUSHY PUDDING!
NICY ICY WATER!

What did you put in your pocket
What did you put in your pocket
  in your pockety pockety pocket
Early Wednesday morning?

I put in a scoop of ice cream
I put in a scoop of ice cream
  slurpy glurpy ice cream
Early Wednesday morning.

  SLUSHY GLUSHY PUDDING!
  NICY ICY WATER!
  SLURPY GLURPY ICE CREAM!

What did you put in your pocket
What did you put in your pocket
  in your pockety pockety pocket
Early Thursday morning?

I put in some mashed potatoes
I put in some mashed potatoes
  fluppy gluppy potatoes
Early Thursday morning.

    SLUSHY GLUSHY PUDDING!
    NICY ICY WATER!
    SLURPY GLURPY ICE CREAM!
    FLUPPY GLUPPY POTATOES!

What did you put in your pocket
What did you put in your pocket
  in your pockety pockety pocket
Early Friday morning?

I put in some sticky molasses
I put in some sticky molasses
  sticky icky molasses
Early Friday morning.

  SLUSHY GLUSHY PUDDING!
  NICY ICY WATER!
  SLURPY GLURPY ICE CREAM!
  FLUPPY GLUPPY POTATOES!
  STICKY ICKY MOLASSES!

What did you put in your pocket
What did you put in your pocket
   in your pockety pockety pocket
Early Saturday morning?

I put in my five fingers
I put in my five fingers
   funny finny fingers
Early Saturday morning.

SLUSHY GLUSHY PUDDING!
NICY ICY WATER!
SLURPY GLURPY ICE CREAM!
FLUPPY GLUPPY POTATOES!
STICKY ICKY MOLASSES!
FUNNY FINNY FINGERS!

What did you put in your pocket
What did you put in your pocket
  in your pockety pockety pocket
Early Sunday morning?

I put in a clean white handkerchief
I put in a clean white handkerchief
  a spinky spanky handkerchief
Early Sunday morning.

    SLUSHY GLUSHY PUDDING!
    NICY ICY WATER!
    SLURPY GLURPY ICE CREAM!
    FLUPPY GLUPPY POTATOES!
    STICKY ICKY MOLASSES!
    FUNNY FINNY FINGERS!
    SPINKY SPANKY HANDKERCHIEF!

Spring

by
Aileen Fisher

When you see a daffodil
and know it's spring,
all the songs inside of you
begin to sing.

The Caterpillar's Story

by
Achim Bröger

One day a small green caterpillar
was quietly munching a large green leaf.
The caterpillar had a large appetite for leaves
and when he had finished chewing up
the best bits of one leaf, he moved on to the next.
Leaves were his favourite food.

Soon the caterpillar had left a pattern on leaf
after leaf as he munched his way up the tree.
On his journey along the branch the caterpillar met
a beetle.

"How lucky you are to have wings," he said.
"I wish I could fly like everyone else around here."
But the beetle flew away without a word
and the caterpillar continued slowly on his way
to the next leaf.

Suddenly he sensed danger and lay quite still,
pretending to be dead. Two birds had landed
on the branch beside him and the caterpillar knew
that if he moved even a tiny bit the birds
would snap him up in an instant. But the birds
just fluffed out their feathers and left him alone.

When they had gone
the caterpillar continued on his leaf-eating journey.

Leaf after leaf, and the caterpillar grew fatter
and fatter. All around him the bees were buzzing,
the mosquitoes were dancing and the spiders spun
their shining webs.

"Oh, how I wish I could fly," said the caterpillar sadly.

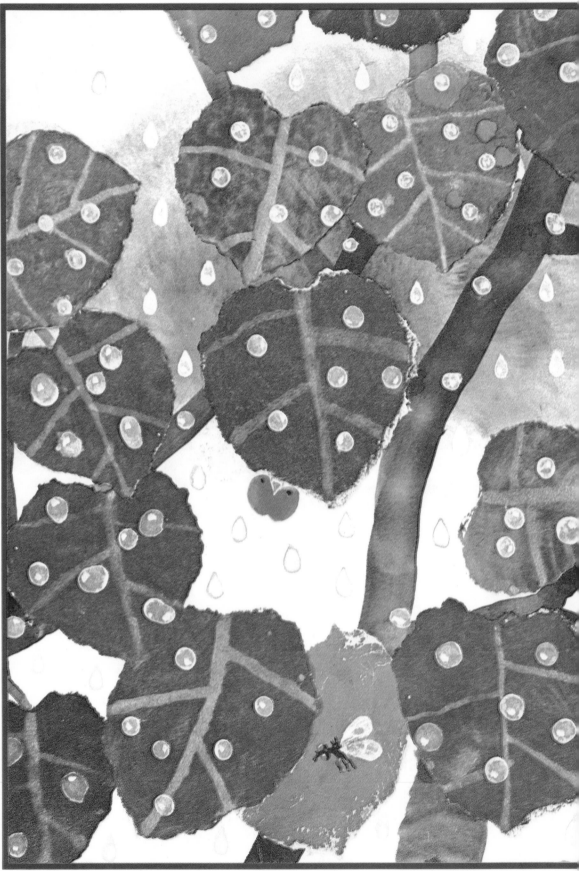

It grew quiet on the tree
and rain began to fall.
The caterpillar took shelter
from the raindrops behind a leaf.
He knew that before long
the rain must stop and the warm sun
would shine again.

When it was fine again the caterpillar moved slowly
from the leaf to a twig, from the twig to a branch
and from there to the wide tree trunk.
The time had come for him to leave the tree.
He looked back at the baby birds who were ready
to leave their nest. He looked at the big tree
that had been his home and theirs.

In the sunshine the bees were collecting honey
from the yellow flowers. Down among the stalks
crept the fat caterpillar, moving even more slowly.

Then the caterpillar stopped altogether.
Slowly he wrapped himself up in a leaf
and went to sleep. The rolled-up leaf lay unnoticed.
Above it the bees continued their search for honey.
The sun shone strongly,
gently warming the strange bundle lying on the ground.
Inside it the caterpillar was changing.
He was dreaming again of flying.

One morning the leaf stirred and split open.
The fat green caterpillar had gone.
In its place was a strange creature with long legs,
and on its head were two long feelers.
Most important of all—it had wings!

The fat green caterpillar
had become a beautiful blue butterfly.
As he soared into the sky,
the butterfly was looking for a partner.
Together they would mate
and lay eggs. Out of the eggs
would come small green caterpillars—
all of them hungry and dreaming of flying.

The caterpillar's story would begin all over again.

Butterfly

by
Wendy Cochran

Butterfly
winging,
dipping,
playing,
darting,
flying,
dancing,
chasing,
soaring,
floating,
wandering,
flitting,
gliding,
hovering,
dashing,
fluttering by!

BOSS for a WEEK

by Libby Handy

If I were boss on MONDAY
in our house,
in our house,
I'd make this rule:

All people living here
coming in from work or
school must change their
clothes IMMEDIATELY!
(NO bare feet either.)

But...

... little Caroline,
sweet Caroline,
neat and natty darlin' Caroline,
may go straight out to play.

If I were boss
on TUESDAY
    in our house,
    in our house,
I'd proclaim:

All people living here
must be inside this
house by five o'clock
ON THE DOT !

        Except for...

    ...little Caroline,
    sweet Caroline,
    prompt and punctual
    darlin' Caroline.
    She may stay out later.

    (Even if it gets a little dark.)

If I were boss on WEDNESDAY
    in our house,
    in our house,
I'd insist:

All people sitting at the
table about to eat
must get up and wash their
hands—and faces too.
(And their knees.)

          EVERYONE except...

... little Caroline,
sweet Caroline,
clean and gleaming
darlin' Caroline.

She may start
her dinner.

If I were boss on THURSDAY
    in our house,
    in our house,
I'd announce loud and clear:

If Dad's got the leftover meatloaf
in his sandwiches for lunch, then...

little Caroline,
sweet Caroline,
hungry, STARVING, darlin' Caroline,
she shall have the same.

(Certainly NOT spaghetti!)

If I were boss on FRIDAY
      in our house,
      in our house,
I'd tell them straight:

All people not having to attend
school tomorrow may stay up as long
as they like and watch television.

Especially...

...little Caroline,
sweet Caroline,
perky, wide-awake,
darlin' Caroline.

(She may
choose the
channel
too.)

If I were boss on SATURDAY
   in our house,
   in our house,
I'd instruct the grown-ups:

No chores for
kids today—
no making beds,
doing dishes,
hanging out clothes
or dusting.

NO
BORING JOBS
DONE
TODAY

Anyway, NOT for...

...little Caroline,
sweet Caroline,
good and helpful
darlin' Caroline.

She needs her rest.

If I were boss on SUNDAY
   in our house,
   in our house,
everyone would know:

WHO gets the wishbone
and the biggest heap
of ice-cream —
two helpings !

Who but...

... little Caroline,
sweet Caroline,
always-eats-her-dinner-up,
darlin' Caroline.

  (And it's not conditional on
  eating her vegetables either!)

If I were boss
for just one week
    in our house,
    in our house,
I'd make them change their ways:
And all for little Caroline,
sweet Caroline,
that golden headed angel,
that paragon of virtue,
that beautiful,
wonderful,
marvellous she,

that dearest darlin', ... , . . . , . . .

. . . . ME!

The Poem
by
Marjorie Weinman Sharmat

Sophie wrote a poem and sent it to Gussie.

> I like your pie
> I like your stew
> But best of all
> I like you.

"What a beautiful poem," said Gussie to herself.
"That poem makes me cry. I'll write one back."

Gussie wrote

> I like your stove
> I like your pot
> I like you best
> Of what you've got.

"Copycat," she said to herself.
And she tore up her poem.

Gussie tried again.

> I like you more
> And more and more,
> Much better than
> Your cellar door.

She tore that up, too.

"I am not a writer," she said. "I'll paint Sophie
a picture."

Gussie painted a picture of a pie and some stew
on a table and Sophie and her smiling at each other.

And she tore it up.

"I'm not a painter either. Now what can I do?"

Gussie thought a long time.

"I know. I'll bake Sophie a thank-you cake."

Gussie got all the things she needed.
She mixed and mixed and mixed.
And stirred and stirred and stirred.
And beat and beat and beat.
And sampled and sampled and sampled.

"This will be my best cake yet," she told herself.

After the cake was baked, Gussie looked at it.

"I hope it tastes as good as it looks," she said.
Then she thought, "What if it doesn't?
What if it tastes terrible? A terrible cake
for a poet? Never."

Gussie tasted a little piece of cake.
"Mmm, good, I think."
She took another little piece of cake.
"Mmm, I really think so."
She took another little piece of cake.
"Mmm. Very good. I'm sure of it."

Then Gussie looked at her cake.

"Oh dear, now it's a used cake. I can't give my friend
a used cake. What can I do now?
I can keep on thinking. Somewhere in my head
there is a good idea waiting for me to think of it.
And I just did. I'll buy Sophie a nice present.
That's what I'll do."

Gussie put on her hat and went to town.

"I'll buy a nice pen for Sophie," she said.
"And a pad of paper. Then Sophie can write
lots of poems." Gussie bought a pad of paper
and a pen and went home.

"I will wrap them in a pretty package."
As she was wrapping the package, the pen leaked.
It leaked over the pad.

"This is not a good pen," she said.
"And now I have a messy pad.
These are not good presents for a friend."

Gussie went to bed with a terrible headache.

In the morning Gussie felt much better.
She went straight to Sophie's house.
"Thank you for the beautiful poem," she said.
And she gave Sophie a big kiss.

Ralph's Dog

by
J. McLeod

My
friend Ralph
has
a smart dog

The dog
can
talk

When
my friend
comes out
the dog shouts
Ralph! Ralph!

(ha, ha)

RALPH RALPH

Howdy!

by
LaVada Weir

Luke was lonesome. He looked out of his window
and watched the people who were waiting for the bus.
No one looked happy. No one smiled.
No one even spoke to anyone else.

Luke climbed up on a chair and got his new cowboy hat
from the top shelf of the closet. Luke put on his hat
and opened the window.

"HOWDY!" he shouted to the people below.

But at that moment the bus roared up to the bus stop.
The people rushed to get on. And the bus roared away.

Luke went to his mother. She was working
at her desk.

"I want to go out with my cowboy hat," Luke said.

His mother smiled, patted him on the head
with one hand, and kept writing with the other.

Luke thought she meant "run along." He went outside.

On the sidewalk, two boys were playing
with a red wagon.

"It's my turn!" yelled one of the boys.
He pulled at the wagon.

"No! It's my turn!" screamed the other boy
and jerked the wagon away.

Luke smiled his biggest smile. He lifted his cowboy hat
and said, "HOWDY!"

The boys stopped tugging at the wagon
and stared at Luke. They were too surprised
to answer or smile back at him. As they watched
the little boy in the big cowboy hat walk on
down the street, the two boys felt foolish.
They began to smile at each other. They were
still smiling when another boy came along.

"HOWDY!" the two boys said. And before long,
they were all saying "howdy" to everyone
and giving rides in their red wagon.

Luke went into an ice cream store.
A girl in a green dress was trying to decide
what flavour of ice cream she wanted.
The man behind the counter said, "Please, little girl,
make up your mind."
Other customers waited.
Everyone was becoming impatient.

"HOWDY!" called Luke, lifting his hat and smiling.
Luke turned and walked out the door.

The people in the ice cream store looked
at each other's faces, and they began to smile.

"HOWDY!" said a little old man in a derby hat.

"HOWDY!" said a tall woman carrying a large sack
of groceries.

Soon everyone was smiling and talking to everyone else. "I'll take vanilla," said the little girl in the green dress. Then everyone else asked for vanilla, too.

The man behind the counter began to whistle a merry tune. The customers were so cheerful that strangers passing by the ice cream store came in to see what was so special. When they were greeted with a smile and a "howdy," they became cheerful, too.

People came out of the ice cream store. Everywhere they went, they smiled and called, "HOWDY!"

Farther down the block, Luke passed by
a gasoline service station. He called out "HOWDY!"
as he lifted his hat and walked on down the sidewalk.

Luke went into a supermarket and walked
up and down the aisles. He smiled and said "HOWDY!"
to everyone he saw.

After he left, everyone looked surprised.
Suddenly everyone in the supermarket was smiling
at everyone else.

Just as Luke was about to turn the last corner
of his block, he heard someone call, "Luke!"

His mother was behind him. She had run
all the way around the block.

"Luke!" she panted. "I have been looking everywhere
for you."

"I wasn't lost. I was lonesome," Luke said.

"How can you be lonesome?" his mother asked.
"I've never seen such friendly people. I followed
a string of smiles and 'howdies' all around the block."

Luke looked puzzled. "Nobody said 'howdy' to me,"
he said.

Luke and his mother came to the steps
of the apartment house.

"HOWDY!" called the people at the bus stop.

"HOWDY!" called a woman leaning out of her window
and watering her flowers.

"HOWDY!" called a group of men
with television cameras.

"See what's happening?" said Luke's mother.

"It must be my hat," said Luke.

"Then your hat works magic," his mother said.

Luke nodded. Then he lifted his cowboy hat, smiled,
and said "HOWDY!" to everyone.

Everyone smiled back.

Luke's mother knew where the magic was.
And she was very proud of Luke.

"HOWDY!"

Split Pea Soup

by
James Marshall

Martha was very fond of making split pea soup.
Sometimes she made it all day long.
Pots and pots of split pea soup.

If there was one thing that George was *not* fond of,
it was split pea soup. As a matter of fact,
George hated split pea soup more than anything else
in the world. But it was so hard to tell Martha.

One day after George had eaten ten bowls
of Martha's soup, he said to himself, "I just can't stand
another bowl. Not even another spoonful."

So, while Martha was out in the kitchen,
George carefully poured the rest of his soup
into his loafers under the table.

"Now she will think I have eaten it."

But Martha was watching from the kitchen.

"How do you expect to walk home with your loafers full of split pea soup?" she asked George.

"Oh dear," said George. "You saw me."

"And why didn't you tell me that you hate my split pea soup?"

"I didn't want to hurt your feelings," said George.

"That's silly," said Martha. "Friends should always tell each other the truth. As a matter of fact, I don't like split pea soup very much myself. I only like to make it. From now on, you'll never have to eat that awful soup again."

"What a relief!" George sighed.

"Would you like some chocolate chip cookies instead?" asked Martha.

"Oh, that would be lovely," said George.

"Then you shall have them," said his friend.

179

In a Dream

by
Meguido Zola

This is a puppy
in a basket
in a bedroom
in a building
in a city
in a world
in a dream.

This is a boy
in a bed
in a bedroom
in a building
in a city
in a world
in a dream.

The Corner

by
Arnold Lobel

Frog and Toad were caught in the rain.
They ran to Frog's house.

"I am all wet," said Toad. "The day is spoiled."

"Have some tea and cake," said Frog.
"The rain will stop.
If you stand near the stove,
your clothes will soon be dry.

"I will tell you a story
while we are waiting," said Frog.

"Oh good," said Toad.

"When I was small,
not much bigger than a pollywog," said Frog,
"my father said to me,
'Son, this is a cold, gray day
but spring is just
around the corner.'

I wanted spring to come.
I went out to find that corner.
I walked down a path in the woods
until I came to a corner.
I went around the corner
to see if spring was on the other side."

"And was it?" asked Toad.

"No," said Frog.
"There was only a pine tree, three pebbles,
and some dry grass.

"I walked in the meadow.
Soon I came to another corner.
I went around the corner
to see if spring was there."

"Did you find it?" asked Toad.

"No," said Frog.
"There was only an old worm
asleep on a tree stump.
I walked along the river
until I came to another corner.
I went around the corner
to look for spring."

"Was it there?" asked Toad.

"No," said Frog.
"There was only some wet mud
and a lizard who was chasing his tail."

"You must have been tired," said Toad.

"I was tired," said Frog, "and it started to rain.

"I went back home. When I got there," said Frog,
"I found another corner.
It was the corner of my house."

"Did you go around it?" asked Toad.

"I went around that corner, too," said Frog.

"What did you see?" asked Toad.

"I saw the sun coming out," said Frog.
"I saw birds sitting and singing in a tree.
I saw my mother and father working in their garden.
I saw flowers in the garden."

"You found it!" cried Toad.

"Yes," said Frog. "I was very happy.
I had found the corner that spring was just around."

"Look, Frog," said Toad. "You were right.
The rain has stopped."

Frog and Toad hurried outside.
They ran around the corner of Frog's house
to make sure that spring had come again.

You'll Sing a Song and I'll Sing a Song

by
Ella Jenkins

You'll sing a song,
And I'll sing a song,
And we'll sing a song together.
You'll sing a song, and I'll sing a song,
In warm or wintry weather.

You'll play a tune,
And I'll play a tune,
And we'll play a tune together.
You'll play a tune, and I'll play a tune,
In warm or wintry weather.

You'll whistle a tune,
And I'll whistle a tune,
And we'll whistle a tune together.
You'll whistle a tune, and I'll whistle a tune,
In warm or wintry weather.

My Friend Jacob

by
Lucille Clifton

My best friend lives next door. His name is Jacob.
He is my very, very best friend.

We do things together, Jacob and me.
We love to play basketball together.
Jacob always makes a basket on the first try.
He helps me to learn how to hold the ball
so that I can make baskets too.

My mother used to say, "Be careful with Jacob
and that ball; he might hurt you." But now she doesn't.
She knows that Jacob wouldn't hurt anybody,
especially his very, very best friend.

I love to sit on the steps and watch the cars go by
with Jacob. He knows the name of every kind of car.
Even if he only sees it just for a minute,
Jacob can tell you the kind of car.

He is helping me be able to tell the cars too.
When I make a mistake, Jacob never ever laughs.
He just says, "No, no, Sam, try again." And I do.
He is my best, best friend.

When I have to go to the store, Jacob goes with me
to help me. His mother used to say,
"You don't have to have Jacob tagging along with you
like that, Sammy." But now she doesn't.
She knows we like to go to the store together.
Jacob helps me to carry and I help Jacob to remember.

"Red is for stop," I say if Jacob forgets.
"Green is for go."

"Thank you, Sam," Jacob always says.

Jacob's birthday and my birthday are two days apart.
Sometimes we celebrate together.

Last year he made me a surprise. He had been
having a secret for weeks and weeks,
and my mother knew, and his mother knew,
but they wouldn't tell me.

Jacob would stay in the house in the afternoon
for half an hour every day and not say anything to me
when he came out. He would just smile and smile.

On my birthday, my mother made a cake for me
with eight candles, and Jacob's mother made a cake
for him with seventeen candles. We sat on the porch
and sang and blew out our candles. Jacob blew out
all of his in one breath because he's bigger.

Then my mother smiled and Jacob's mother smiled
and said, "Give it to him, Jacob dear."
My friend Jacob smiled and handed me a card.

Happy Birthday Sam
Jacob

He had printed it all himself! All by himself,
my name and everything! It was neat!

My very best friend Jacob does so much helping me,
I wanted to help him too. One day I decided
to teach him how to knock.

Jacob will just walk into somebody's house
if he knows them. If he doesn't know them,
he will stand by the door until somebody notices him
and lets him in.

"I wish Jacob would knock on the door,"
I heard my mother say.

So I decided to help him learn. Every day
I would tell Jacob, but he would always forget.
He would just open the door and walk right in.

My mother said probably it was too hard for him
and I shouldn't worry about it. But I felt bad
because Jacob always helped me so much,
and I wanted to be able to help him too.

I kept telling him and he kept forgetting,
so one day I just said, "Never mind, Jacob,
maybe it is too hard."

"What's the matter, Sam?" Jacob asked me.

"Never mind, Jacob," was all I said.

The next day, at dinner time, we were sitting
in our dining room when my mother and my father
and I heard this really loud knocking at the door.
Then the door popped open and Jacob stuck his head in.

"I'm knocking, Sam!" he yelled.

Boy, I jumped right up from the table
and went grinning and hugged Jacob,
and he grinned and hugged me too.
He is my very, very, very best friend
in the whole wide world!

Hush, Little Baby

Traditional Canadian

Hush, little baby, don't say a word,
Mama's going to buy you a mockingbird.

And if that mockingbird won't sing,
Mama's going to buy you a diamond ring.

And if that diamond ring turns to brass,
Mama's going to buy you a looking glass.

And if that looking glass gets broke,
Mama's going to buy you a cart and yoke.

And if that cart and yoke turn over,
Mama's going to buy you a dog named Rover.

And if that dog named Rover won't bark,
Mama's going to buy you a horse and cart.

And if that horse and cart fall down
You'll still be the sweetest little baby in town.

Kate's Secret Riddle Book

by
Sid Fleischman

I hope you don't have a friend like Wally. He lives across the street. Wally is always doing mean tricks. And then he flaps his arms like a dumb chicken and laughs.

On Saturday he rang our doorbell.
"Let me in, Jimmy," he said.

"No," I said. "My sister is sick."

"I want to tell her a riddle. It will make her laugh."

I hadn't been able to make Kate laugh all week.

"Do you want to hear a riddle?" Wally asked.

"No," Kate said.

"It's a funny riddle."

"Well, okay," Kate said.

"Ready? Here's the riddle. Doggone!"

I said, "That's not a riddle!"

"It's the answer to one. You've got to think of the question. That's the funny part!" said Wally.

He flapped his arms like a chicken. He laughed all the way out of the house.

"I feel sick," Kate said.

"You're already sick," I said.

"I feel sicker. He'll never tell us the riddle."

"Maybe someone else knows it. I'll be back," I said.

I met the mailman at the front door.
"Do you know any riddles, Mr. Hunt?"

Mr. Hunt scratched his head.

"What did the fly say when he fell
into the melted butter?"

"Doggone," I answered.

"Nope," he said. " 'Look! I'm a butterfly.' "

At the store I asked Mrs. Mitchell,
"Do you know any riddles?"

"Let me think. If you put a clock
in a beehive, what time would it be?"

"I give up."

"Why, it would be hive o'clock." Mrs. Mitchell smiled.

I helped Mr. Snow out with his bags.
"Do you know any riddles, sir?"

"Of course I do. If ducks say 'quack-quack'
when they walk, what do they say when they run?"

"Doggone?" I asked.

"They say 'Quick! Quick!' "

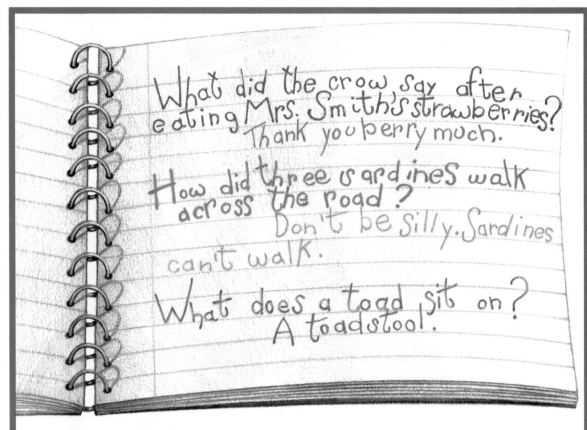

Maybe Wally had made up that crazy answer.
But it gave me an idea. I ran back to the store
and bought a small school pad. I'd write down
all the riddles I heard before I forgot any.

Just about everyone I met had a riddle to tell me.

What did the crow say after eating Mrs. Smith's
strawberries?
Thank you berry much.

How did three sardines walk across the road?
Don't be silly. Sardines can't walk.

What does a toad sit on?
A toadstool.

The book was almost full when I saw Miss Smith.

"Oh, I know a riddle," she said.
"What side of a house gets the most rain?"

"I don't know, Miss Smith."

"The outside."

I wrote it down. Just then something happened
across the street. Mr. Cross's dog got out of the yard
and ran away. Mr. Cross gave an angry shout.

And I gave a whoop. I knew the question
to Wally's riddle!

I wrote it in the book. On the cover I printed
"KATE'S SECRET RIDDLE BOOK."
I ran home as fast as I could.

Before long Kate was laughing so hard
that Wally could hear her. He came to the window.

"What are you laughing at?"

"Your riddle," Kate answered. "Doggone.
Wally, that's the funniest riddle in the whole world."

"It is?" Wally said.

"I can't stop laughing," Kate said.

"Tell me the first part," begged Wally.

"Oh, you know it."

Wally said, "No, I don't. I just made up
that doggone answer to tease you. I don't know
the question."

"You're just pretending," Kate laughed.
"Oh, it's so funny. But don't worry.
Jimmy and I promise to keep it a secret."

"Come on and tell me," Wally said.

"You're looking kind of sick, Wally," Kate said.
"You'd better go home to bed. Goodbye.
I'm feeling so much better."

She held up the book and read the last riddle again.

July

by
Fran Newman and Claudette Boulanger

Lie on your front in the summer sand;
Bake for as long as you can stand.

Lie on your back, let the heat soak in;
Then roll around on your summer skin.

Lie on your side to enjoy the view;
Ease yourself over to toast side two.

Run to escape the blazing sun. . . .
It's too late—you're overdone!

Under the Shade of the Mulberry Tree

by
Demi

Once, long ago, there was a rich man
who lived in a house by the side of the road.

The house was shaded by a stately mulberry tree.
Every day the rich man sat in the shade of the tree
and went to sleep.

One afternoon a poor man came and sat down
under the tree. The rich man did not like this at all.

"Get up, get up, get up," he shouted.
"You can't stay here!"

"It is so pleasant here," began the poor man,
but he was interrupted.

"This is my tree," shouted the rich man.
"I own all of it: the trunk, the branches,
the leaves and the shade. Everything!"

"I cannot possibly buy all that," the poor man thought
to himself. "But I might be able to afford the shade,
and that might be even better."

"Will you sell me the shade?" he asked.

The rich man was delighted that there was money
to be made.

"Why not?" he answered quickly, thinking the poor man
was a fool. He called to some people passing by
to help them agree on a price. After sharp bargaining,
the shade was sold.

Every day after that the poor man came to sit
under the tree to rest. Wherever the shade
happened to be, the poor man followed.

Sometimes he rested with his bull.
Sometimes he reclined in the rich man's sitting room.
And often he invited his friends and their mules
to rest in the shade too.

One day the rich man sat at his table
in the shade of the mulberry tree eating with guests.
The poor man entered, with his water buffalo,
and sat down at the table.
When the guests learned he had bought the tree's shade,
they laughed out loud.

A day came when the rich man could stand it
no longer.

"How dare you intrude like this into my courtyard,
even into my house. Get out! Get out! Get out!"
he screamed.

But the poor man continued as before.

This was too much for the rich man to bear.
He moved away to another house
where there was no shade.

The poor man
moved into the rich man's house altogether,
bringing his animals with him.

But he never turned away anyone
who wished to sit and rest
under the shade of the mulberry tree.

August Afternoon

by
Marion Edey and Dorothy Grider

Where shall we go?
   What shall we play?
What shall we do
   On a hot summer day?

We'll sit in the swing.
   Go low. Go high.
And drink lemonade
   Till the glass is dry.

One straw for you,
  One straw for me,
In the cool green shade
  Of the walnut tree.

Alligator's Sunday Suit

by
Priscilla Jaquith

One day long ago,
Alligator was floating in his home creek
thinking how fine life was.
In those days, he would always dress up
in a white suit good enough for Sunday.
He lived in the water with all the fish he could eat,
so he never had to work for a living.
And he never, ever met up with trouble.

Well, Alligator was enjoying a lazy time in the hot sun, when Bo Rabbit came hopping along the creek shore.

"Good morning, Alligator. How are you today?" said Bo Rabbit, stopping to pass the time of day.

"Doing just fine, thank you kindly. How is everyone at your house?" said Alligator.

"Oh, we're getting by. But we have so much trouble, Alligator, so much trouble," sighed Bo Rabbit.

"Trouble? What's that?" said Alligator.
"I've never seen trouble."

"You've never seen trouble?" cried Bo Rabbit.
"Great Peace! I can show you trouble, Alligator."

"I'd like that, Bo Rabbit.
I'd surely like to see trouble," said Alligator.

"All right," said Bo Rabbit. "Meet me
in the broomsage field tomorrow morning
when the sun has dried the dew off the grass,
and I'll show you trouble."

Next morning, when the sun was high,
Alligator took his hat and started to leave the house.
Mrs. Alligator asked him where he was going.

"I'm going to meet Bo Rabbit
so he can show me trouble," he said.

"Well, if you're going to see trouble, I'm going too,"
said Mrs. Alligator.

"Oh, hush!" said Alligator in a high and mighty voice.
"You'd better let me go see trouble first.
Then I can show you."

That made Mrs. Alligator very angry.
She wanted to go see trouble right away.
Alligator and Mrs. Alligator quarreled so loudly
that all the little alligators heard them
and came sliding into the room—

 hirr, hirr, hirr, hirr, hirr, hirr.

Then the little alligators began to holler,
"If you're going to see trouble, we're going too.
If you're going, we're going too!"

They made such a racket that,
just to save his poor ears,
Alligator finally roared, "Quiet!
All right! All right! You can ALL come."

They crossed the marsh and by the time they got
to the broomsage field, there was Bo Rabbit
sitting on top of a stump waiting for them.

"Good morning, Bo Rabbit," they said.
And all the little alligators made little curtseys,

sazip, sazip, sazip, sazip, sazip, sazip.

Bo Rabbit said "good morning" back.
"You have all come to see trouble, is that it?" he asked.

"That's it," said Alligator.

"That's it," said Mrs. Alligator.

"That's it," said all the little alligators.

"All right," said Bo Rabbit. "Stand out
in the middle of the field and wait.
I'll go get trouble and bring it here."

Alligator, Mrs. Alligator, and all the little alligators
slithered into the field—

*KAPUK, Kapuk, kapuk, kapuk, kapuk, kapuk,
kapuk, kapuk.*

Bo Rabbit ran to the far edge of the field
and cut off a little handful of broomsage.
Then he set fire to it and ran round
and round the field until the fire was everywhere.

Mrs. Alligator saw the fire jumping, hot and red.
She saw the smoke rising.

"What is that, Alligator?" she asked.
She had never seen fire at home in her wet marsh.
Alligator looked around and shook his head.
He did not know.

"I think that's the trouble
that Rabbit wanted to show us," said Mrs. Alligator.

All the little alligators jumped up and down
and hollered, "Isn't trouble pretty, Ma?
Isn't trouble pretty?"

But soon the fire got hotter and the fire got closer
and the smoke got so bad that all the alligators
had to flee to the other side of the field.
The fire caught up to them!

They turned and ran another way.
The fire caught up to them! The fire got so close
that it felt like it was going to burn them.
They all shut their eyes and threw their heads
close to the ground. Then they dashed through the fire.
They didn't dare stop until they reached the creek.

Alligator jumped in—*SPASHOW!*
Right behind him was Mrs. Alligator—*Spashow!*
Then all the little alligators jumped in—

spashow, spashow, spashow, spashow, spashow, spashow!

All into the creek!

As they scrambled out, Bo Rabbit watched them
from across the stream.

"You've seen trouble now, Alligator. Would you like
to see it again? I can show you," he hollered.

"NO SIR, Bo Rabbit, NO SIR!" cried Alligator.

Alligator looked at his suit. His beautiful white suit,
good enough for Sunday, was gone. Now his suit
was blackish-green and rough and bumpy.

"It's all Bo Rabbit's fault," said Alligator.
"Him and his sneaky ways!"

But even as the words came out of his mouth, Alligator knew in his heart that HE had asked to see trouble.

"I have learned one lesson for all my life," said Alligator. "Don't go looking for trouble, because you just might find it."

And as for Alligator's suit, it is blackish-green and rough and bumpy, even today.

Coin Puzzlers!

by
Jack Booth and Jo Phenix

Over and Under!

Instructions: Put a quarter on a table or desk.
                        Put a penny beside the quarter.

Rule: Do not touch or move the quarter.

Problem: Put the penny under the quarter.

                  Here's how!

Pick up the penny.
Hold it under the table, beneath the quarter.
The penny is now under the quarter!

For a Change!

Problem: How many different ways can you make change for a quarter?

Here's how!

There are 12 ways!

2 dimes, 1 nickel
2 dimes, 5 pennies
1 dime, 3 nickels
1 dime, 2 nickels, 5 pennies
1 dime, 1 nickel, 10 pennies
1 dime, 15 pennies

5 nickels
4 nickels, 5 pennies
3 nickels, 10 pennies
2 nickels, 15 pennies
1 nickel, 20 pennies
25 pennies

X-Ray Eyes!

Instructions: Put a coin "tails" side up on a desk or table.
Place a sheet of paper over the coin.

Rules: Do not move the paper.
Do not touch the coin.

Problem: Read the date on the coin.

Here's how!

Hold the paper still.
Use the side of a pencil point.
Rub it gently on the paper, over the coin.
You will see the date!

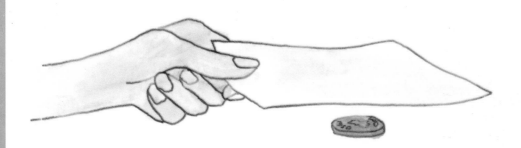

Which Is Quicker?

Instructions: Put your hand on your shoulder,
with your elbow pointing out
in front of you.
Balance a penny on your elbow.

Rule: You may not use your other hand.

Problem: Swing your elbow down.
Catch the penny before it hits the ground.

Here's how!

Be quick!

Rhymes Without Reason

Traditional

Here I am, little jumping Joan;
When nobody's with me,
I'm all alone.

The grand old Duke of York,
He had ten thousand men;
He marched them up to the top of the hill,
And he marched them down again.
And when they were up, they were up,
And when they were down, they were down,
And when they were only half-way up,
They were neither up nor down.

Hector Protector
was dressed all in green;
Hector Protector
was sent to the Queen.
The Queen did not like him,
No more did the King;
So Hector Protector
was sent back again.

Higglety, pigglety, pop!
The dog has eaten the mop;
The pig's in a hurry,
The cat's in a flurry,
Higglety, pigglety, pop!

Diddle, diddle, dumpling, my son John,
Went to bed with his trousers on;
One shoe off, and one shoe on,
Diddle, diddle, dumpling, my son John.

How Anansi Brought the Stories Down

A Folktale from West Africa

by
Barbara Winther

Characters

THE STORYTELLER
NYAME, the Sky-god
ANANSI, the Spiderman
CROCODILE
MONKEY

STORYTELLER: I am a storyteller from a village
in Africa. I am going to tell you a story
about Anansi, the Spiderman. Anansi is a sly,
clever spider. For this is his way of living
among larger, stronger animals. The story I will tell
is called "How Anansi Brought the Stories Down."

SETTING: Forest of Africa, Kola nut tree
and berry bush are near centre. Hornets' nest hangs
from bush, and calabash gourd is on ground.

STORYTELLER: It all happened near the beginning
of time, not long after animals were on the earth.
Anansi thought it might be fun to tell stories
in the evening. But Nyame, the Sky-god,
was the owner of all the stories.

NYAME: Here comes Anansi, climbing into my sky.

ANANSI: Good day to you, Sky-god.

ANANSI

Storyteller

NYAME
THE SKY GOD

ALLIGATOR

MONKEY

NYAME: All my days are good, Anansi.

ANANSI: But of course. It is only we poor earth creatures who have bad days.

NYAME: I'm not going to change that. If that's why you've come, go home.

ANANSI: No, I'm here for another reason. I want to buy your stories.

NYAME: What? Buy my stories? You dare climb into my sky and ask me to sell you my stories? Great kings have tried to buy them. My stories are not for sale.

ANANSI: Don't be angry with me, Sky-god. I'm just a little spider trying to make my way in life. Isn't there any way I might talk you into giving up your stories?

NYAME: What a bother you are.

ANANSI: Why? Because I don't give up easily?

NYAME: Oh, all right, Spiderman. If you can show me a crocodile with no teeth, an empty hornets' nest, and a quiet monkey, I'll give you my stories.

ANANSI: Sky-god, there are no such things.

NYAME: But if you're as clever as some say, then you can make them. Now, go away. I must plan the weather for next week.

ANANSI: A crocodile with no teeth,
an empty hornets' nest, and a quiet monkey.
That will take some doing.

CROCODILE: Hungry! Hungry! I'm so hungry
I could eat anything. I'm only happy
when I'm eating more and more.

ANANSI: I have an idea! Say, Crocodile,
I know where you can get a meal.

CROCODILE: Where, where, where?

ANANSI: Over there.

CROCODILE: I don't see anything
but a big, green rock.

ANANSI: I see a plump juicy frog that looks like a rock.

CROCODILE: Yum, yum! A plump juicy frog. I see it now. That frog is trying to trick me into thinking it's a rock.

ANANSI: Why don't you sneak up quietly on that rock—I mean frog—open your mouth wide, and snap your jaws shut as hard as you can.

CROCODILE: That's just what I'll do. Yum, yum! Ouch! That's the toughest frog I've ever eaten!

ANANSI: Aha! Did you see that, Sky-god?

NYAME: Yes, Anansi. Greed broke the crocodile's teeth. Now, find an empty hornets' nest.

ANANSI: Ah, there's a hornets' nest. But it's full of hornets. This calabash gourd looks almost like a hornets' nest. That gives me an idea. Hornets, hornets, your home is too small. See this? I've brought you a bigger, more beautiful home. Just take a peek and see how much better off you'll be in here. Aha! Did you see that, Sky-god?

NYAME: Yes, Anansi. Dissatisfaction emptied the hornets' nest. Find a quiet monkey and my stories are yours.

ANANSI: This is going to be the hardest job of all.

MONKEY: Chitter, chitter, chatter. Look how pretty I am. Chitter, chitter, chatter. What a perfectly gorgeous monkey I am!

ANANSI: I have an idea.

MONKEY: Hello, Anansi. Is something wrong with you?

ANANSI: It's not possible. It simply can't be done.

MONKEY: What can't be done?

ANANSI: There's a great reward for the animal who can stuff its mouth with twenty kola nuts and still talk.

MONKEY: Twenty kola nuts? Like the ones on this tree?

ANANSI: Yes, and no one can do it.

MONKEY: What's the reward?

ANANSI: The animal who can do it
becomes king of the jungle for a week.

MONKEY: Oh, oh, oh! I must have that reward!

ANANSI: But you can't do it.

MONKEY: Yes, I can. Just watch me.

ANANSI: Excellent! Excellent! Now talk to me. Did you see that, Sky-god?

NYAME: Yes, Anansi. Vanity made the monkey speechless. I see you understand the ways of the world, Spiderman. From this day on, the Sky-god stories will be known as yours.

Anansi

**by
Bert Simpson**

Anansi, he is a spider.
Anansi, he is a man,
Anansi, he is a lazy one,
do little as he can,
yeah, do little as he can.

Anansi has a mango tree,
He loves the fruit so ripe.
He cannot reach the mangoes
but he longs to have a bite.

So, Anansi tells his friend the crow,
"You're beautiful to me."
Old crow calls her friends,
so they can hear his flattery.

The crows fly to the mango tree,
they bend the branches down.
Anansi watch them swing and sway
and mangoes hit the ground.

Anansi, he is a spider.
Anansi, he is a man,
Anansi, he is a clever one,
he always have a plan,
yeah, he always have a plan.